DC LANFRANCHI

Future in Safety

The Blue Book of HSE

DC LANFRANCHI

Future

In

Safety

The Blue Book of HSE

Future in Safety

Copyright 2019

www.resiliere.com

Published by Deborah Lanfranchi

Amazon Kindle Direct Publishing.

16395 words

First Edition

September 2019

ISBN 9781709031458

I dedicate this, my third book, to the future potential of my whole family, to my husband, Juan Martín, and my children, Santiago, Camila and Lucía. I also dedicate it especially to my parents, Yolanda and Néstor and to my ancestors, because at a time, I was also their future.

Finally, I dedicate it to all those with whom I shared my passion and my mission. I deeply wish they feel proud and empowered with my humble contribution to help build a joint vision of a better world.

Creating a better future implies to learn from the past and to be thankful for the knowledge acquired, while at the same time, we work for it at present with passion and commitment.

INDEX

Prologue

Nowadays, the focus of the future of Corporate Social Responsibility is clearly on safety and health and on the inclusion of these issues in professional training and reflection programs, both as regards the role of new technologies as well as its impact on the new economies.

Consequently, the future leads us to talk about break-through innovation and technology, mindset change and the development of new economies. For this, it is necessary to refer mainly to Singularity University. SU was founded by, among others, Ray Kurzweil, one of today's brightest minds, with doctorates from more than 10 universities and hundreds of inventions and patents. He has been granted several awards by the Massachusetts Technology Institute and received many honorary recognitions. Ray Kurzweil is a real visionary.

Singularity University encourages the union between the man and the machine. In fact, the concept of Industrial Safety deals with the relation that there is or will be between the man and the machine, that is to say, how technology becomes an integral part of the personal protection elements, and how they will relate

and work together in the future. That is why we will talk about Cobots.

In the automotive industry, 80% of the activity is carried out by robots, and human beings provide these robots with raw material. No doubt then, that Singularity will be the main actor in the future of Industrial Engineering Safety.

We must pay special attention to the Singularity of Things over the next 10 years. We cannot go on thinking that personal protection elements will not be connected to automated and systematized networks monitored by men and machines.

Today, at home, we have 7 or 8 devices connected to the net, but in the next 10 years we will have from 1,000 to 2,000: refrigerators, lights, cameras, taps, toilets, air conditioning, everything.

This is the road that is being built today and we are heading in this direction. No doubt about it. However, whether this will take 10, 20 or 30 years depends only on the political economy. But it is already happening. It is similar to the eighties when the PC appeared and revolutionized the market.   Singularity, quantum computing and other things are changing the market and the world.

About twenty years ago I read of book by Ray Kurzweil, *The Age of Spiritual Machines*, where he portrayed future scenarios. The number of subjects he dealt with and participated in personally is immense.

Why do I associate Singularity University, Ray Kurzweil and this book? Because I agree completely on the idea of training to develop a future with a brand new and revolutionary leadership, as regards corporate social responsibility, safety and change management. Lanfranchi reminded me of its great importance and I saw an evident alignment between Deborah´s vision and mission and the vision of those supported by Singularity from its beginnings.

I am really enthusiastic to encourage those who dream of and pave the way to the future. Only a few of them are bold enough to do it.

In the case of Deborah´s book, the objective of which is to spread the message of the importance of safety and the reduction to zero accidents at the workplace, we find a very interesting, easy and quick reading introduction to the subject of the future of safety. The objective of the book is to raise individual and collective awareness on the real importance of Safety and to show the tools to learn and implement new safety practices.

After reading the first two books by Deborah, *"Leadership in Safety"* and *"CSR in Safety"*, I felt attracted by her new book, which deals with the future of safety. A preliminary version of *"The future of Safety"* got to my hands, and I really enjoyed reading it. When she invited me to write her prologue, I was very keen on starting it immediately.

What I liked especially about this book is her vision of the five senses, as well as her approach and the emphasis on the importance of measuring.

I invite you to read this book and be surprised. I also discovered that its reading can be complemented by sailing on the internet the interesting tour suggested by Deborah. This book is a motivator, it encourages, challenges, drives us to discover new solutions with a look on the future.

Just a few books had this effect on me. Today I feel the urge to place Deborah's books in my library, next to Ray Kurzweil's books, next to the books on conscientious leadership, and next to those by Stephen Covey, Benjamin Graham, Dan Senor and Saul Singer, Elon Musk, Gates Foundation, and some other important reference material which guides me in my duties as businessman and stockholder.

Global Workplace Safety Director

October

2019

Preface

In the year 2019 I knew I was about to break fresh ground: moving from my corporate responsibility for generating safety to a new area which includes working as a consultant and trainer for leaders in safety at organizations and the public in general.

On this new road, I discovered that the most direct way to generate value, to transmit my vision and to train in safety is by writing books and holding workshops. These books are written both in English and Spanish to suit the needs of customers from different cities around the globe.

I started writing about the most basic and fundamental matters in order to achieve deep change. The first book dealt with Leadership in Safety, the next one with Corporate Responsibility and the fourth with the change management required for the satisfaction of these goals. To identify what needs to be changed, it is essential to talk about the future of safety, and this is the subject matter of my third book.

My books are organized in 3 sections: Anticipating, Taking Action and Measuring. Their objective is to guide the reader in the learning process of the different concepts, and in the internalization, implementation and evaluation of the different subjects treated in each book.

In my first book, I developed the subject of Leadership in Safety, and I introduced the concept of gradualism and uninterrupted work to achieve sustained results.   Good leadership implies and ensures high performance in safety, eliminating completely any risk caused by distraction, excess of trust and ineffective communication.

In my second book, I went over the issue of our social responsibility as businessmen and I talked about sustainable acts as regards resources, future generations, and the human being and their complexity. In this book, you will also find a summary of the universe of standards and sources related to safety and corporate responsibility.

In this one, my third book, I analyze the future of Safety.   We will go deeper into today's needs and international safety trends, which will undoubtedly result from innovation in technology and leadership. For this reason, R K's vision, Singularity University (SU), appeals that much to me, as I work in radical innovation and state of the art technology applied to knowledge and at present, also in safety.

Likewise, I deem it convenient to mention and thank two people. One of them is Roberto Reduello, Global Workplace Safety System and Process Automation Manager in General Motors, who leads safety practices of over 250,000 employees in tens of countries, who used to be my boss when I started my career and who instilled in me the importance of being practical and down to earth and focusing on the reduction of accidents metrics everywhere, by means of working in the present with our minds set in the future.

The other person who generously authorized me to mention him, is Tim Kinsella from Manson Constructions, ESOP Company (with Stock Ownership Plan for employees), classified within the 400 best Engineering

Contractors in the United States. Thanks Tim for sharing with me the mission you lead for Manson, which is a 100% committed to encouraging a zero accidents culture, following the guidelines you have defined in five steps: 1) Training 2) Planning 3) Personal Safety Elements 4) Commitment and 5) Communications.

This book invites leaders to get to know what is coming, to become aware and go over the multiple and diverse subjects relative to Integral Safety for organizations and for individuals and thus to create, for all, a better future.

I invite you to press the white button to start.

Introduction

In 1970 in the United States, around 20 million people worked in Safety. Today, 50 years later, this number was reduced by a half. Similarly to what happened in the areas of Human Resources, where technology has decreased the number of employees, promoting self-management. This process is also taking place in the area of Safety. This decrease of human capital also results from the merger of positions, as a consequence of which many managers broaden their generalist skills, absorbing roles such as "Human Resources Business Partner", "Safety Business Partner", and many other transversal positions.

When I think of innovative technology and its scope as regards Safety, I am inclined to ask, Should technology focus on adding a sixth sense to the five senses we already have? Or, should technology focus on supporting the senses we already have, and in a certain way, improve them? My answer is that it should focus on both.

How will technology impact on safety? In industrial safety, on the one hand, it is important to put on the table, the relevance cobots (collaborative robots) have and will increasingly have in the future and also the potential of augmented reality, different from virtual reality. The first one increases visual capabilities, the second, changes the reality of what we see.

All the population will use technology to enhance their senses and we will undoubtedly witness that protection elements will follow suit. Protection will be foreseen, but new functions will be included to modernize and even ***transform*** senses!

This book invites leaders to explore what comes. I write this, for it is essential to perceive the years to come to be able to work in the present. As I repeat in my teaching activities, we must be more efficient in reducing potential future accidents.

In all the books I develop a 3-step methodology, called ATAM.

1) *Anticipating*
2) *Taking action*
3) *Measuring*

Anticipating is to look into the future, and to anticipate we need to be practical. That is it includes the following issues:

- Safety in the cobots´ era.
- Training and augmented reality.
- Artificial Intelligence and training
- Singularity University. Ray Kurzweil.

In **Anticipating**, I will write about the five senses and I will deal with it in the following chapters:

- The human being as adjusting agent at the workplace.
- Protective elements and the five senses.
- Hearing and earmuffs.
- Touching and gloves.
- Smelling and masks.
- Sight and eye protectors.

- And what about taste?
- The helmet, a separate issue.

In **Measuring** I will deal with:

- Technology and lone working.
- Broadcasting needs.
- Legal Updating Needs.

Likewise, I would like to emphasize that we are driven by our passion and enthusiasm, and that we see the future as something very close to us, even if in some areas change and evolution have been more gradual. Especially, as regards accidents at the workplace, we have not achieved the zero accidents vision yet, which would ensure that our employee, relative or friend got home sound and safe after a day at work. After having gone over these pages, the reader will count with several elements to achieve the goals of zero accidents and total safety.

PART 1 ANTICIPATING

Lanfranchi´s 2030 vision of ZERO INJURIES AT THE WORKPLACE

In this book, I intend to state the vision I wish for the future. For the year 2013 I hope that every employee who is responsible for people has a certification in Leadership in Safety with ZERO INJURIES at the workplace vision.

Writing a book about a better future, supposes to work at present with a strict vision of the future. Even today, each year there are millions of accidents and I intend to help reduce these injuries, this pain, year after year, to achieve zero injuries.

In this book I share everything I have learnt about the development of science. This development, sometimes require changes that we, as individuals, do not welcome.

At my lectures and workshops, I emphasize that the main tool we have to anticipate injuries is our mind. It is our processor, due to the fact that it remembers experiences and builds patterns that protect human life. This includes our ability to generate solutions and create new processes, and so we can conclude that, if the mind perceives something as real, then it is real.

The subjects of the future, safety and health, are subjects on which many important and influential people are working. It is very inspiring to see Bill and Melinda Gates´ foundation striving to eradicate deaths caused by

Poliomyelitis or daily hygiene. The method they use to analyze geographical behavior patterns is similar to my methodology with which I seek to eradicate injuries at the workplace. I am interested in reading, how Alphabet, the owner of Google, inspired by Ray Kurzweil, is studying the development of artificial intelligence to create a mind able to produce thoughts, called by some people, the Rosetta Stone, which helped decipher ancient languages.

In line with this, we find individual and collective imagination, as if it were a big broadcasting network sending messages to all its members. This is necessary at the workplace: to share perception.

The best way to anticipate to the future is by creating it. That is why I undertake to work on the training of general skills that will reduce accidents, supported by technological advances, the development of metrics in spread sheets as well as to encourage the creation of patents for personal protection elements.

The importance of soft skills for the future

Business Skills for the future

Every professional must develop skills to understand and develop business challenges. Every skill may have a huge impact. Skills should also be developed to see businesses from an innovative perspective. For example, all the intellectual property assets do not constitute any expense at all, but an increase in the corporation´ s capital. They represent a source of income . For example, to contribute with a patent for gloves recycling in the automotive industry also adds commercial value to the organization.

The challenge of workers´ daily life in particular, and of individuals in general, is to start performing their task in a quieter and better organized way and without a hurry, and without being busy all the time. We should work on the other end of technical skills, called soft skills, based on empathy. This implies to understand what we and the others know, need and feel and to work on this, so that we can achieve the best version of ourselves towards a common goal.

In a program for the reduction of accidents, we will surely find that it takes years to develop a complex procedure to diminish them, and this is why this book acquires relevance and why it is essential to define ourselves with our eyes set on the future.

Attitudes needed for a more technological future

As regards safety, we must work on the events and circumstances that cause stress, one of the most common causes of accidents. Everything that brings about a bad attitude and/or a bad posture clearly indicates we should pay more attention to this situation.

Which circumstances cause stress? The main one is the lack of anticipation. For example, the change of a leader produces healthy uncertainty, thus, I include here some recommendations to have a better attitude

- Introducing new people to current working mates. For example, we can place a screen on a wall, with visual information about all the employees, old and new, fostering interaction, via the inclusion of tastes, interests, situations and leisure activities common to all.

- Continuous Training. Knowledge brings about peace of mind and this knowledge must be practical.
- Using virtual reality technology to study a building and simulating stressful situations to learn how to cope with them.
- Developing a positive attitude, full of gratitude and respect. Saying thank you and please, smiling and keeping eye contact, might seem to be trivial things, but it is demonstrated that once acquired, these attitudes significantly diminish stress symptoms.

I could mention many more, but I prefer you to choose them and elaborate periodically at your workplace, your own list of factors diminishing stress. Doing away with stress is a non-ending task and it should be encouraged because it is closely related to the quality of life and the reduction of accidents.

Communication of the future

OSHA standards, among others, explained in detail in my book CSR in Safety, are only the tip of the iceberg. What is seen is controlled, what is measured and set as a procedure can be controlled, but we still see, for example 38% of misunderstanding in oral communication.

In the year 2030 there will be more communication, much more than today, partly between men and machines. There will be more oral interaction, as we can observe today on our telephones or smart gadgets, when we talk to Siri or Alexa or to the different virtual agents.

<u>We will have to foresee oral communication among devices,</u> it will not be surprising to find a device addressing an audience made of human beings and machines at the same time.

The importance of language

With globalization and the changes in economy, a new distribution of activities is being introduced, and together with this, we find that some risky tasks are carried out by workers who do not speak the language of the country where they are working and do not have access to training in this language.

In big corporations, some enforceable standards of voluntary application such as ISO standards are audited, as well as OSHA regulations or similar ones, depending on the country, but in some small corporations the impact they have on the environment is ignored. Due to this, we notice in the events prior to an accident the acts of people without the corresponding knowledge or training, not only on the part of in-company staff, but of outsourced personnel as well.

There is a common saying that may come in handy in this context, which states: "prudent people have accidents because of imprudent ones".

Generally speaking, for a medium sized company with 150 to 200 employees, it might be more complicated to comply with the standards or requirements imposed by big companies, even more difficult for small or sole proprietorship businesses. In these cases, cooperation with their customers is important, because big and small sized companies can cooperate synergically.

All of us are the future. Public and Private Sectors

Many safety professionals look for a job in the private sector, convinced that they may find more benefits or labor stability in the face of political changes.

What really encouraged me to write about this subject in the 2030 vision was my participation in the Annual Awards Ceremony of the United States National Safety Council in September 2019 in San Diego, California.

At this ceremony, where Lorraine Martin, President of the Council, handed in more than 150 awards, I was surprised to notice the importance given to awards received by government members such as firefighters, police officers, and staff of the armed forces and the army.

The reason is obvious. For them, safety is a critical part of everyday life and they have developed discipline and habits which are and will be even more valued in the private sector. To fulfill their duties, they focus on the importance and observance of physiology, the basis of a healthy body. Then, good physiology is a critical factor of success in reducing accidents.

This explains why government officials provide significant cooperation to the private sector, contributing with healthy habits that minimize injuries.

I would be delighted to see more firefighters, police officers and members of the forces receive training in engineering, industries and to see them working more in HSE and CSR areas.

Cooperation in the future

In the year 2030, we will observe over a 50% reduction of people performing tedious or repetitive tasks, and more robots/cobots/agents cooperating. There will be an increase in integrated and collaborative working opportunities, because they encourage productivity growth. But new tasks will also be found among these new technological agents, such as the monitoring of automaton programming and data analysis. Consequently, there will also be an evolution in management processes. But for this to be successful, sound knowledge and good practices are fundamental to achieve a high percentage of efficiency in their implementation.

Today, while this book is being written, we can observe that many occupational accidents, mainly in the industrial sector, take place in the area of motor vehicles, and we observe at the same time, a sustained growth of autonomous vehicles. This growth in automation will reduce accidents, since the connection of devices, vehicles and any kind of product and service will increasingly help set the algorithms for the prevention of accidents.

The prevention of accidents based on data analysis will contribute to differentiate the "necessary" information from the "unnecessary information", resulting in more efficient planning.

Let's see an example.

Many people might wonder: how can a vehicle in motion stop before a potential accident to be caused by other means of transport? One solution might be to stop the offender who is about to cross against the light before this event takes place. And, how?

Well, if both vehicles are connected to a data network using cooperative algorithms to monitor in real time the speed of the vehicle and if the data network is also connected in real time to the network of traffic lights, then three actions could be easily carried out:

a) *Foreseeing that the vehicle slow down its speed (this would be the concept of dynamic and flexible maximum speed allowed in real time, which changes the maximum speed allowed in real time).*
b) *Anticipating to changes in traffic lights to achieve the reduction of vehicles speed.*
c) *Planning direct communication with the security forces to stop the vehicle that is not respecting traffic signs.*

How to do this? Especially in Safety, it is appropriate to ask this question to oneself. It is necessary to be quick in anticipating and for this, it is important to count with quick data processing and clear communications. The answers "I cannot", "it is not possible", "I would like, but …", are solved with a greater calculus processing power.

Main difference between information and data

Further information processing technology

How is it possible to increase processing power and multiply it exponentially to enable all the serves operating in 2019 fit into a small room? The answer is provided by quantum computing.

It is not a dream or science fiction. Google, Microsoft, Intel, IBM, Hewlett Packard already have computers using this new technology.

Even if I am explaining this later on, I would like to introduce a bit of information on how quantum computing seems to be the answer. Quantum computing does not work with bits 0 and 1, but with qubits, which handle more states, developing exponential growth computing instead of linear ones.

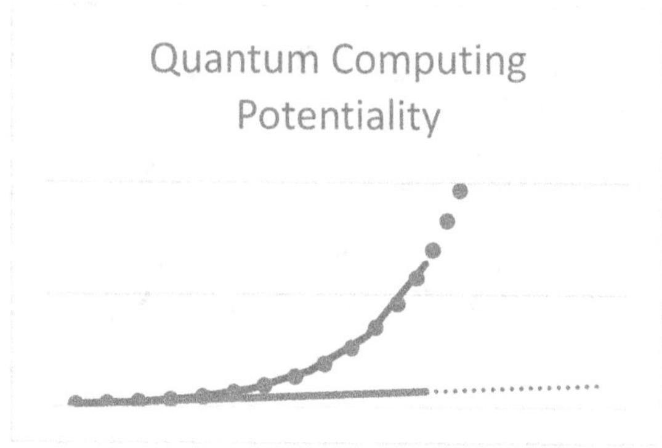

Specialists, Generalists and new technologies

In 2030 we will still have specialists in different fields and subjects. Yes, we will, but they will also possess generalist skills. And what is the advantage of this? Given that specialists know and deal with subjects and different fields in depth, they are very important for the correct management of business. But, it will become increasingly necessary to count with general knowledge of different areas, because the information obtained from quantum computing cannot be implemented by specialists. For them, it will only be data. A specialist and generalist professional will consider it key information.

As has been stated before, we are witnessing an important change as the result of the decreasing number of workers in many areas of industry, while at the same time there is an increase of workers in other areas of this ecosystem.

Where today there is a single position, due to the complexity of the future, there will be tens and hundreds of new associated jobs.

Progress generates new technologies and this brings about the creation of new materials, products and service ecosystems.

We are moving from a society that manufactures products and raw material to a society that generates services rendered by these products. Likewise, environmental challenges also increase, and together with this, there is also a growth of CSR positions which work on the workplace ecosystem.

If this service grows and people waste time due to injuries and diseases, it is then necessary to cover generalist aspects of new technologies absorption. Winners anticipate, losers only react. Due to this, it is imperative to study the impact of new technologies on our activities.

In the future, those responsible for safety will have to work together with those in charge of providing suppliers and customers with a safety ecosystem at the workplace. I foresee that 20% of their time they will have to work together with people from other companies, and I also predict that they will share workplaces. That is to say, if we are responsible for the safety of a place, we will need to have enough room so that outsiders, such as suppliers can share information with us.

The future will need generalists. No doubt, we will need HSE professionals who will also be able to play other roles, to name a few: production, data analysis, health, environment, medicine, finance, etc. Within this context, it will be essential to have knowledge on mathematical calculus and spreadsheets.

To sum up, technology has always changed the way we work, and this will continue happening at a greater speed and with more complex contributions, for which we need to train seriously apart from improving our flexibility.

The importance of surveys starts in anticipating

Surveys are extremely important when we need to know what we have to anticipate. Results will then acquire meaning when the moment comes to take action and measure.

For surveys to prove really useful, it is fundamental to distinguish when they provide useful information and when they do not. Even today, we still see surveys and forms where employees are asked to rate from 1 to 10 an activity, a benefit or a risk. Later, as illustrated by the graph below, we will make an account of the data obtained.

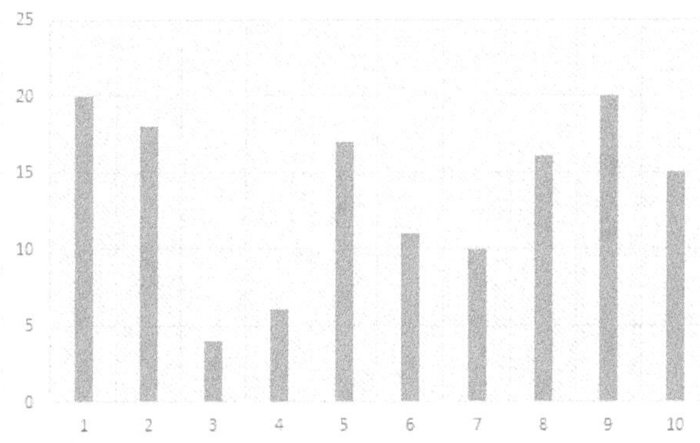

As we only give options from 1 to 10 we do not offer the chance to assess a situation negatively, but only from neutral to positive. If 1 is equivalent to "very bad", this figure can be considered negative. This will only be the interpretation of a person, but it is not like this for a computing mathematical function. From the point of view of mathematical evaluation, for the right and finite processing of data, we need negative numbers, because they, together with positive numbers, offer real information not mere data. That means that, with the same people population, we can offer numerical answers, but also the negative evaluation of an activity. If we enlarge the scope of answers from -10 a 10 we add a unique and unrepeatable value, the 0, the neutral state of an answer, neither negative nor positive. In mathematics the figure zero has no sign, but in informatics adding a sign would show the trend of a neutral value. This is known as critical factor trend.

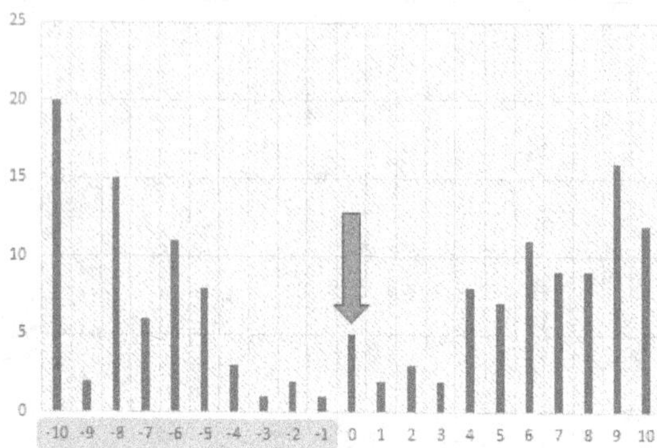

With the same population, looking for associations of combined answers, we find a different kind of result.

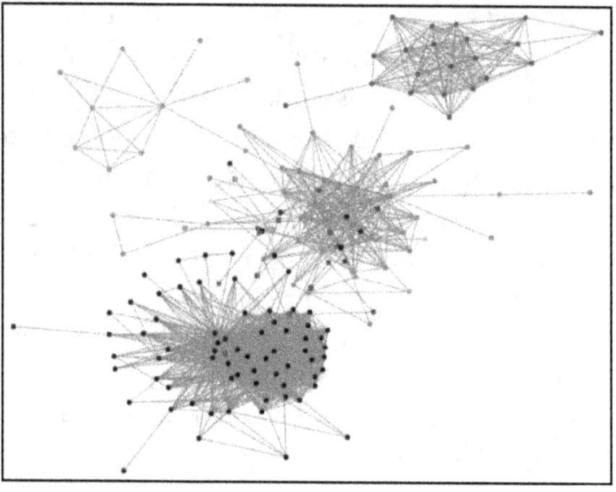

For surveys results, I suggest using methodologies which include negative assessments. This will make it easier for service industry executives to fully notice the risks faced by their people and their assets, such as cobots.

The importance of technology in safety in the era of cobots

The image of the cities of the future where everything is robotized and the coexistence of men and machines belongs to everyday life, has already got to our workplaces. Needless to say, some tasks and places do not allow men to be replaced by machines. But there are others that, because they are risky, lack humanity, and imply physical and/or mental effort would rather be replaced by cobots.

A cobot is a collaborative robot which has been created to work with human beings. It is essential that in the XXI century the tasks to be carried out by people are decent and correspond to those to be performed by human beings in all respects (connected with CSR in Safety).

In the laboratory SLS (Spoken Language Systems, of the Massachusetts Institute of Technology (MIT), communication interfaces with human beings are studied. The true challenge at the beginning of the year 2000 was the development of virtual agents which work at the same time and in parallel, crossing information from different sources. We could orally ask which the nearest address of a store is, while looking at a map at the same time. Two data entries had to be processed, the question in a natural language and the human interface pointing at a location. This is not a real challenge, because the efficiency of answers is related to the power of calculus processing and algorithms.

The real challenge appears when this interface takes place among cobots where a human being participates as a third party, or in the relationship between two human beings where a cobot assists both of them. Disambiguation of communications among different sources is a complex problem of scarce resources.

We can have an automation process established, but what is not foreseen is the environment where this automation process will take place. Each facility is different. Those in charge of safety, will then become more aware of the relation of the events of the various parts of the system to analyze, either human or automated.

Here lies the base of future safety. There are many people studying how to talk to a machine, but there are not so many investigating how machines can talk to one another.

Let´s see the case of nanobots. Nanobots are robots at a nanometric scale which are necessary for chemical analyses, especially to measure toxic chemical concentrations in the environment. A nanobot must have for ability to build a copy of itself, which includes the means to find the necessary raw material.

Why would we wish to have a self-replicating machine? It would be fundamental, for example, to build solar cells to do away with fossil fuels and to place them in highly polluted areas or areas that cannot be reached by human beings.

We clearly see that the challenge of automation is not only communication with a human being, but communication among them and the methodologies to recruit, train and complete these computerized auxiliaries.

It is important to guarantee that this interaction is as much coordinated as possible, for a cobot is not more than a machine that moves.

Quantum Computing

The idea of quantum computing appears in 1981 when Paul Benioff explained his theory to take advantage of quantum laws in the realm of computing. Instead of working with electrical voltage, he invited to work with digital computing, a single bit can take two values: 0 or 1. Whereas, in quantum computing, the laws of quantum mechanics participate, and the particle can be in coherent superposition: it can be 0, 1 and 0 and 1 at the same time (two orthogonal states of a subatomic particle). This allows several operations to be carried out simultaneously, according to the number of qubits.

The number of qubits indicates the quantity of bits that can be in superposition. With conventional bits, if there were a record of 3 bits, there were eight possible values and the register could only take one of these values. Whereas, if there was a vector of 3 qubits, the particle can take eight different values simultaneously thanks to quantum superposition. Thus, a vector of 3 qubits would allow a total of eight parallel operations. As can be deduced, the number of operations is exponential to the number of qubits.

In the same way in which I have recognized the source of inspiration offered by Raymond Kurzweil, I want to mention another person of Soviet origin, not so popular, called Nikolai Brusentov, who developed the first computer called Setun, with ternary base, that is to say, not using bits 0 and 1, but three states. This computer was created in the Soviet Union in 1958, and I consider it a source of inspiration for many people who worked in quantum computing.

Moore´s Law (1964), developed by Gordon Moore, cofounder of Intel, forecast that integrated circuits that are developed remain unalterable for 24 months, that is to say, that approximately every two years the number of transistors is duplicated in a microprocessor. Afterwards, there follow a chain of inventions that generate new and different circuits. This law is still in force and it is a real mystery why this happens in this way. Anyway, this kind of growth is represented by a linear trend curve.

Instead, quantum computing is exponential, so we are likely to have by the year 2030, computers with a capacity millions of times superior to the capacity of current computers. This would enable calculus processing, which will in turn, make it possible to foresee, given previous planning and in real time, every potential accident.

Let´s see another example of Singularity. If in the future, we want to avoid falls from height, a valid option would be that harnesses consider the singularity of combining an element of personal protection, such as the harness, the helmet, etc., with automated characteristics to make work more comfortable and efficient. For instance, a harness, a pair of gloves, a helmet or any other personal protective element could be "connected" to a data network and they will **jointly** transform a complex problem, in a system of simple problems **combined** among them.

Artificial Intelligence and training

Emerging trends in technological advance, such as big data, cloud computing, artificial intelligence, robotics, 3D printing, simulators and the convergence of technology (biotechnology, nanotechnology, information technology and cognitive sciences) are creating new opportunities and challenges in all realms of life, including safety at the workplace.

To ensure industrial safety, we need to introduce solutions based on artificial intelligence, which will be able to pinpoint and learn to deal with different types of risks, to tackle them and provide solutions to avoid its occurrence.

The "2030 Thought" will make some working environments safer and will turn the current industrial safety standards obsolete. The new interaction between man-machine in a workshop must also observe healthy and safe practices. And last but not least, future technologies must prevent cyber attacks.

Augmented reality, virtual reality and the impact on training

Augmented reality is in my opinion, one of the most powerful technological advances of this century.

It has a characteristic that makes it enormously convenient and of easy and creative implementation. Every translucent material (windows, doors, floors, roofs, machine coatings, clothes, lenses, containers, etc.) which due to their transparency, let the light pass through, but which block environmental elements such as noise, wind, water and insects, animals and people movements, is a potential element to complement augmented reality.

Augmented reality has many uses. The use of augmented reality as a training tool is an enriching element for experiences, highly appreciated in good training. It is known that every experience we feel in our body is an experience that lasts over time, so that is why I consider it important to use this kind of virtual tool to achieve a unique experience. In general, it is very difficult to explain which the consequence of neglecting a procedure might be, or which could be the consequence of an accident. It can be intellectualized, but it is very difficult "to feel" an electric arc discharge or to imagine how it feels to fall from a high place. This technology draws these experiences closer to our senses.

For example, using a rendering by means of augmented reality, would enable us to see, on a screen, at real time, the dangers inherent to the workplace derived from the plan of the building or from the production lines of a company and use it for its own employees.

Training Proposals

"Our own experience is very expensive and arrives late" as the saying goes. How can I teach offering these experiences? Suppose a fatal accident takes place and causes the death of a worker in front of an electric board, or behind equipment moving materials. Can we use simulation in the same way as airline pilots use it in simulation cabins to train risky situations? Of course, we can. I personally lived that experience. Below you will see pictures I was taken while trying augmented reality technology related to safety. To do this, I was placed in front of a board, in a virtual scenario provided by the company Nextwave Safety Solutions Inc.

These training solutions are relatively easy to develop. Every company has the engineering plans of plants, so it is not complicated to recreate the scenery of these plans in a virtual rendering, and afterwards develop training programs specific to each plant. To this end, it would be advisable to know beforehand the facilities, to observe them, to walk them thoroughly, and especially to observe if there are changes in the plans compared to the real facilities at that time.

In the first place, I recommend installing this technology, in order to implement it in a place where a fatal accident has already taken place, if this is the case, or where a many injuries have previously occurred. We can also analyze and share metrics with other organizations considering our population sample, the sample complement or the market sample.

Where can I train?

We should clearly get training in three areas:

- Training in Safety, Standards and Regulations.
- Training in the organization, adjusted to our circumstances.
- And training in the impact of automation and singularity.

Singularity University

There is wide training available, especially in standards. Universities offer post graduate courses in industrial safety, but I would like to describe the importance of Singularity University in detail. This University was founded by, among others, Ray Kurzweil, one of today's brightest minds. His accreditations are many, such as doctorates in more than 10 universities, awards from the Massachusetts Institute of Technology and many more honors. Undoubtedly, we can say Ray is a gifted visionary.

Recently I learnt that R. K. follows an incredible diet consisting of 250 pills a day and more than 6 intravenous transfusions with nutritional complements. I was and I wasn't surprised at the same time, given his level of inventiveness and commitment. I personally consider him an incredible person, whose infinite curiosity transforms every subject he deals with. Nor was I surprised to learn that he has created hundreds of inventions and patents.

Just to name a few, Ray Kurzweil has developed one of the first systems of character recognition (OCRs), the first scanner with artificial intelligence algorithms, the first text to speech synthesizer, the first synthesizer to reproduce piano and orchestra sounds and technology related to human being senses and artificial intelligence.

In Kurzweil's words, the singularity of our future is clearly defined as the destiny of cooperation between machines/technology and human beings.

After exhaustive study and investigation, I believe that it is in this singularity where we will find the key and the foundations to achieve zero accidents.

Following SU guidelines, we can infer that every personal protective element should be "connected" to a data and analysis network. Imagine a helmet that allows us to monitor a lone worker, or footwear that allows us to track the movements of each employee at a plant in the same way as the position of every shot is analyzed in a basketball match.

This singularity will enable us to go beyond the biological boundaries of our bodies and mainly of our senses, enhancing our individual capabilities and connecting them cooperatively.

Let's see one more descriptive example. Imagine the game Rubik, which consists in ordering the six color cube, made of 9 little cubes per side (there are various models with more cubes per side and different sizes and designs). Now suppose that some "cubes" (components) are biological, and that they correspond to human beings′ characteristics, and other "cubes" (components) are automated, typical of an improvement process. How can we measure the singularity of the combination of the elements? We will be able to measure this combination when we have understood that singularity is like having a Rubik with one cube only, everything integrated.

PART 2 TAKING ACTION

The human being as adjusting agent at the workplace

An agent is an entity that renders a service. Within the context of workplace change, an agent is the one who has, and undertakes whole responsibility for communicating and managing this change.

For this reason, to manage change and to reduce accidents, we must consider each individual as an agent for this change. A leader's responsibility does not only entail to manage change, but to communicate it and focus on it. Change management requires team work and mutual cooperation.

At an industrial plant, there are many situations in which the human being is taken or used as an adjusting variable, that is to say, it is the only entity within the organization with constructive capabilities to adjust to complex situations, urgent decision making, difficult layouts, etc.; while cobots, robots and machines cannot do it, due to their inflexible structure and design.

It is in these situations, where most occupational injuries and diseases occur, where anticipation arrives late and human beings are obliged to deal with them instead. Here, stress, unhealthy or unnatural postures, blows, etc, come into scene.

It is here where I consider technology has to be at the service of men's wellbeing, helping predict these risky situations and potential diseases. It is here that cobots come into scene accompanied of a transformation process of jobs or tasks. The person accompanying the cobot will carry out a new task, never done before. These will generally be tasks that require enhanced thinking quality and knowledge. People will have to think more and will do less repetitive and/or forced movements.

Musculoskeletal disorders and other pathologies

As defined by the National Institute for Occupational Safety and Health (NIOSH) occupational musculoskeletal disorders include injuries of muscles, tendons, ligaments, nerves, joints, cartilage, bones or vessels of arms, legs, head, neck or back caused or increased by work related activities such as lifting, pushing or pulling objects. Symptoms may include, pain, stiffness, swelling, numbness and/or tingling.

I ask this question especially to those in charge of safety: Was there a history of musculoskeletal disorders in the cases involving fatal accident? This question includes the person or group of people who were victims of accidents and fatalities.

Working in the employees´ physiology is also vital. Disorders can be avoided using ergonomic assistive devices.

I advise to integrate the database of people´s medical appointments to the database of informed injuries. For example, hypertension causes occupational accidents if the incident is related to work. "How can it be related to work if the individual hardly sleeps 8 hours and the rest of the day he lives and works in a stressful job which impacts on every area of his life?" —I strongly state at lectures and workshops. Continuing with the example of hypertension (there could be many other pathologies) we can state that, it is either directly related to a determined and objective activity or indirectly to a subjective activity (psychological impact).

In order to analyze further the importance of stress and its psychological impact, I invite psychologists to my new lectures, to help understand the origins and consequences of chronic occupational stress. I advise all who may be interested in this subject, to carry out multidisciplinary consulting activities. If you own or conduct a plant, the visit and monitoring of a psychiatrist may prove to be highly advantageous, since this specialist can observe habits from an angle completely different to the one of an engineer.

Motor Vehicles

As stated in the data platform Injury Facts, trends are not prophecies, but they indicate the direction of collective behavior. The number of accidents and injuries caused by motor vehicles in the year 2017 was 4,7 million in the United States, with an approximate cost of 433 billion dollars. Over 40,000 people died in an automotive universe of 270 million vehicles registered in the USA.

Fatal accidents are caused in most cases in motor vehicle drivers or passengers.

The critical analysis factor is then in transportation moments, and I consider that whether these moments were planned or not should be added to the analysis.

I do insist then, how can we decrease the number of accidents? Providing a singular working environment beforehand, acquired from better training of human personnel and efficient cooperation of technology.

I strongly believe that an accident and, mainly fatalities caused by a motor vehicle, are predictable. People approaching vehicle circulation areas must wear a bracelet on their wrist, with a system such as Near Field Communication, which interacts at short distances and produces a specific signal, for example a vibration, to warn a worker of any potential risk. Likewise, this same bracelet, which is connected to a database, when "realizing" the increased potentiality of an accident, that is to say, when it registers a risky pattern, can change color and warn the worker involved in such activity. It can also be the gloves they are wearing, or the eye or ear protector or the helmet. The use of technology in clothes is an important element to be used as a preventive method.

Ray Kurzweil in his 1999 book, "The Age of Spiritual Machines" already mentioned that by the year 2019 computers would be among everyday elements in the same way as clothes, furniture, jewelry and especially inside our bodies.

Protective elements and the five senses

When I visited the National Safety Council in 2019, I was surprised to find many stalls exhibiting a wide variety of personal protective elements. Day after day, there will be more products with new proposals, due to the protection requirements workers will have to observe in the future. We will have to work hard to offer PPEs, more and more comfortable, more modern, more friendly, more technological, and why not, more fashionable (remember the case of Cocó Chanel, who was a pioneer when she brought fashion to postwar workers outfits in the United States).

Personal protective elements should incorporate technology, especially to enhance our physical potential, not only to protect it.

The combination of elements and technology is essential. A pair of gloves that changes temperature according to the material it feels, enhances touching, even wearing gloves. A recording on a screen attached to a helmet increases information, by means of augmented reality. Bone conduction headphones can cause vibrations, which transmit sound without blocking hearing canals, adding two new hearing canals to the human body.

It is imperative to consider protection and the enhancement of our senses, as well as working conditions, cold protective clothing, fire protective clothing, work at height and every variation required by the different tasks, focusing on zero accident policy.

Hearing and earmuffs

As regards hearing protection, one of the most important factors to be analyzed before choosing the appropriate protective element is the reduction of decibel levels to which a person is exposed.

When environmental noise exceeds 85 decibels, hearing protective devices are needed, to maintain the recommended maximum limit for normal hearing. In these cases rubber earplugs, or earmuffs are used.

This protection diminishes harmful noise, but at the same time blocks hearing and can even distort perception and equilibrium. The good thing about these protectors is that they prevent harm to hearing. The bad thing is that it does not allow us to hear the warning of a work mate who might be alerting us of an imminent risky situation. This kind of protection disallows an extremely important channel of information to the brain.

I had the opportunity to get to know the company Aftershock, pioneer in bone conduction technology, with more than 300 patents developed so far.

I found it very interesting to use these headsets in combination with protective rubber earpieces to protect ears, as it enables us to hear sounds through our eardrums and bones simultaneously.

In this way, if workers use this kind of headset with a microphone capturing environmental sound and voice, then we could make use of a second pair of ears to hear our workmates or bosses. The challenge might then be to reduce background noise in communications, and to provide technology which synthesizes sound more efficiently.

The singularity of our future is already present in our daily life. There are people who wear headsets the whole day connected to their devices and mobile phones. Children and adolescents spend more time wearing headphones than hearing environmental sounds.

Using this personal protective device as a communication collaborative assistant ensures the reduction of accident risks.

In an organization, I was asked how to implement the change to connected headsets for their thousands of employees. I answered that the change was not necessary because this is already taking place with the mere existence and daily use of cell phones. We just have to manage the interaction among these devices, we do not need to introduce new ones, at least at the beginning.

We should also bear in mind that people are used to wearing headphones due to the use of cell phones, either to communicate, keep informed or listen to music, and because of this, many people are worried about preserving their healthy hearing. Interviewing hearing specialists, I learnt that people are increasingly adopting Britzgo amplifiers, or that they are incorporating "Audio Zoom" technology, which reduces noise smartly. This is used for example, in filming sets to improve the sound of the person being focused over background noise. The problem of audio amplifiers is that they amplify all the environmental sound, making it necessary to use calculus processors.

In 1976, Ray Kurzweil released "Kurzweil Reading machine", first reading machine for the blind capable of translating printed material into spoken words. This information triggered the following question. Is it possible to develop reading procedures for material and sensors and send them as audio material to people? With the new trend of processing chips we will be able to give a headphone the capacity possessed by thousands of computers simultaneously.

Touching and gloves

One of the elements increasingly present in protective elements is gloves. There are many types, with different characteristics, functions and appearance.

There are latex antibacterial and antifungal gloves, which are ideal to handle chemical substances and for health purposes. Some are made of synthetic materials more resistant than latex and combined, that is to say that they may have different types of protection, such as protection against cuts, pulled threads, abrasion and holes depending on the mostly affected zones. And there also were gloves against extreme temperature, cold or hot, others for dry or wet places, some more comfortable as polyurethane gloves for wrapping procedures and electrical components handling, others for welding, and so on. As you can see the variety is immense.

It is very interesting to see how companies incorporate technology to gloves. From GPS devices to assign gloves use to a specific point, such as 3 axe gyroscope sensors, near field sensors, environmental light sensors, temperature sensors, barometers, speedometers, and many other types of sensors that are being released to the market on a daily basis.

I would like to share a thought with my readers about gloves. The gloves of the future should not prevent us from the huge capability of feeling what we have in our hands. We can perceive a rough surface and only touching it can we determine the degree of danger it possesses. If we wear gloves, this capability is impaired and we change it for the assumption originated in a single or combined circumstance of temperatures and situations.

Gloves must be equipped with sensors and must enhance the anatomical characteristics and the sensitive and motor capabilities of our hands.

In the relation among the size of phalanges we can find Fibonaccils´ sequence, and in the relation between the forearm and the hand, we will find PI number (∏). Nails can also evidence the health of a person, among many other data given by our hands and arms. That means that glove providers in the future will be experts in safety, ergonomics, health and technology.

Smelling and masks

The main concern of people in charge of safety as regards smelling and masks is to protect the respiratory tract.

The inhalation of oxygen and the exhalation of carbon dioxide via a good breathing process constitute the energy input and output system needed for the correct function of the human body. Any alteration of the air we breathe produces infinite conditions and problems, some of them immediately, other in the long term.

The protection of smelling is provided by masks that filter or conduct air. This is achieved thanks to devices we carry with us; but masks may cause many inconveniences.

During a visit to a plant some years ago, the person in charge of the guided tour gave me a filtering mask, because the tour included sectors which required the protection of our respiratory tract.

As we walked and talked to different people, we

needed to move the mask with our hands outwards to keep on talking.

When the visit was over, I met with the plant chief and I asked him what the use of wearing a mask was, if we had to remove it every time we wanted to say something.

These are the questions I ask to myself when I notice that the personal protective element in question inhibits people anatomy and basic capabilities.

My opinion today is that at places where masks are worn, collaborative devices based on technology should be introduced. In the case mentioned before, wearing a mask without the adequate complementary headsets and microphones originates risky situations, the exposure to unhealthy products and some more which together constitute a big problem of trust for the development of corporate safety. If we do not use protection in the correct way, we increase the occurrence of situations leading to occupational accidents or disease.

Sight and eye protection

In a working environment, sight provides us with basic and relevant information as regards safety. Consequently, any personal protective element is absolutely essential.

Sight enables me to see through translucent material, so I can have a material between my sight and the object I want to see. This will allow me to use this material to protect and to see information by means of augmented reality technology. The translucent object can reproduce a screen, and so if I superpose the screen to my sight, I will obtain what is called an augmented vision, augmented reality.

Protective eyewear is ideal to incorporate augmented reality. From technologies providing data to a specific and fix area of vision, to providing dynamic information, which appears in different places of the vision surface related to the focus shift when a new element is seen, or to the visual field change when moving.

Eyewear protection must offer visual recognition data. Can I recognize a person and project data about this person in my vision?, about a machine?, about an electric board?, about an order?, stock changes?, maps?, information outside my angle of vision?, for example, to my back, similarly to car cameras when they go in reverse?. I absolutely can.

What kind of hazards can I identify with information on a screen? Color shifts in protective elements due a sensor attached to objects affecting the respiratory tract? I also can.

So, let's see which 3 elements the protective eyewear of the future must have:

a. **Protection.** It must protect sight from all sorts of blows and situations that might impair vision.
b. **Information**. It must give information of people, machines and real estate that helps us with our task, as well as of processes and states that help achieve enhanced productivity.
c. **Sensors**. It must contain all sorts of sensors, because visually, it is very easy to distinguish an alarming situation.

I go on thinking and I add the following: Can images be directly projected into the retina? The answer is yes, but it does not have commercial use yet, because these technologies and their applications are still under investigation at the moment this book is being written in the year 2019.

In Redmond, Washington, there is an enterprise called MicroVision, which is part of the group of high technology leaders in the metropolitan area of Seattle. MicroVision is a pioneer in laser beam scanning that allows the creation of miniature projection screens with high resolution and sensors.

 Guided by my passion of reading and knowing the latest trends and technological adventures on board of which human beings are; I found myself thinking: we have to be practical! I see enterprises trying to manufacture miniature screens while others manufacture bigger ones, but I conclude that, sooner than later, we will be projecting screens on walls, floors and translucent windows!, of which we will be able to choose the size we want, depending on any given circumstance or need.

Then, if we are talking about taking action, providing a 440 workers shift with a helmet with a visor and headphones that amplify hearing capabilities while protecting health, helmets with screens, harnesses, and helmets with tracking devices and routine analyses, gloves that improve touching while offering protection, constitute clear actions towards a radical change. But I know this might require planning, assessing, testing, and investing, to name just a few. But, if we really want to act towards a zero accidents future, why don´t we start with small things, as for instance the automation of walls, doors, stairs, roofs, floors, windows?

Data projection can be dynamic according to the population with which we interact.

Should we then incorporate screens to walls? Yes! But first I´d rather recommend installing projectors, they are easily moved, screen sizes are flexible, they are easily maintained and cheaper.

I would start, individually, to carry out pilot tests of some specific functions.

For instance, as regards the use of rendering in training rooms for workers who need to have access to complex and dangerous areas in the plant to offer them virtual and rendered training.

And what about tasting?

Especially in the field of food quality control, there is a complex relation between taste cells and chemical sensors.

Salinity in areas close to the sea, is perceived by experts via smelling and tasting, and this is the reason why it is very important to determine chemical components of the air and of food individually and on a permanent basis. Once again, the combination of technology and the human body is necessary.

I frequently hear that it is impossible to detect the immense quantity of information processed by human beings through taste, and my answer and advice is to start perceiving changes.

If I have a chemicals sensor and for 200 days the results of different analyses follow a mathematical pattern, but one day, this pattern changes, it will be easy to identify changes in raw materials, in recipes or even in the product quality.

The detection of movement or living organisms is also one of the qualities we can perceive with taste.

The senses of tasting and smelling are intimately linked. When we put on a protective mask, not only do we inhibit smelling, but also cancel tasting. Sometimes a trace contaminant is first discovered at the mouth, at the tip of the tongue and then with the nose. If we add to this that we are also impairing hearing with the use of hearing protection and sight with protective eyewear, we are practically eliminating the five senses human beings need to survive and communicate with the world outside them.

Many fatal accidents occur because the perception of the contaminant risk did not take place with the due anticipation needed to take action and save lives.

I remember the example of a rescuer of some Thailand children who had been isolated after a Monsoon. The news said that the rescuer had run out of air … but I deduce that there was a failure in all the alarm systems which should have warned that the level of air in his tanks was decreasing. Due to the fact that the whole natural system of protection, that is, his senses which are the best detection system, was completely disrupted and blocked, the rescuer was not able to notice the imminent danger he was in.

Smart clothing with sensors

When choosing working gear, we should take into account the risks workers can face. To this end, we should choose the kind of gear that best reduces risk. Working gear should not be prone to getting caught by machines in movement, but if this does occur, clothes must be easily torn so that workers can be immediately freed from this situation. This means that it must be, at the same time, but under different circumstances, resistant and weak. Unfortunately, I have visited various plants with different lines of business where fatal accidents occurred due to the fact that working gear, which is supposed to guarantee workers' safety, proved to be themselves the elements which caused their death, because somebody got trapped in a machine that finally killed him.

A huge challenge lies ahead of us, to incorporate cell phones, devices which have already been incorporated since the year 2007, to almost all our activities at home and at work.

As the use of the working gear supplied by the enterprise is compulsory during working hours, it is then very simple to add technology to clothing.

We can already consider the idea of wearable cobots.

Many of the technologies we have mentioned and which we consider necessary to achieve zero accidents rate, are at present being studied. And until technologies are developed and tested by leading enterprises that highlight the importance of people's safety in their agendas, I am afraid they will be just this, issues under exploration, investigation and testing.

DuPont contributed with many patents to clothing technology as regards chemical treatments to fabrics and materials discovered as protection against fire, cuts, etc. In my opinion, today a new chapter starts with sensors and wearable technology by which sensations can be connected, for instance: cold sensation releasing an exothermic reaction inside the components of the fabrics itself generating heat.

I estimate that many hours have to be spent on a chair to incorporate knowledge, development and technology to the task of providing a worker with safe clothing.

The helmet, a separate matter

I will devote some time to go over the subject of the helmet in depth, for it is a broad subject in itself. As has previously been mentioned, it would be easy to incorporate to the helmet a camera and sensors with different accessories, such as a GPS to monitor task in real time, or to use this information in dynamic projections on walls, visors, monitoring or training rooms.

Head protection entails multiple variants. It may be an industrial helmet, a cap or net as in hospitals or cleaning services, or a hat for kitchen staff, which prevents hair from falling on food.

Helmets protect head against trauma, falls, dangerous objects, chemical aggressive substances, electric current, etc. Plastics turned out to be of great use, and if we incorporate harnesses inside, they can also become highly beneficial to soften impact and trauma.

But let´s resume the analysis of the other important functions of helmets. The most important information it can provide is its physical location in real time. Metrics of these 2 variables combined enable the analysis of risk anticipating behavior, since the helmet must analyze and report location, change, impact and any other information relevant to the safety and health of people by means of sensors.

If a cell phone today has 3 axis gyroscope sensors, speedometers, proximity sensors, ambient light and barometers, in the same way as other commonly used devices, have color sensors which indicate distances travelled, speed and pulsations and many more, so it becomes evident that we have to study deeper how to use helmets and the existing and future technologies to ensure safety at the workplace.

As far as communications is concerned, it is vital that we can communicate with the helmets via devices, program them and allow them to program themselves. On a rainy and humid day, programmed sensors may interchange information on humidity levels in walls, floors, rooms and machines.

The helmet must be communicated to drones. The use of motion in monitoring devices is essential, for we always have to analyze the presence of mathematical patterns which are not present at analyses.

A drone bearing hydrogen fuel has autonomy for over 2 hours, allowing the intensive study of pipes leaks, escapes, smoke focal points and so on.

In work at height, a helmet that has network communication and informs the height the person is at, will allow us to transmit and verify the presence of other complementary safety elements for this task, such as holding harnesses.

PART 3 MEASURING

The scope of measurements

Five-minute rule

If performing a measurement analysis takes us longer than expected, then it will prove to be a discouraging activity.

In surveys, I always hear people say they do not want to waste time in analyses. This is why I recommend Lanfranchi's 5 minute law. If it takes me more than 5 minutes to analyze metrics, then they are not metrics but mere data. It is essential to reinforce the fundamental difference between what is useful and what is useless. Analyzing metrics is very useful because it provides us with information in less than five minutes. Whereas, it is difficult to understand what useless data provide, and therefore they cannot be used in anticipation implementation.

If in the directory of my computer, I have a spread sheet previously prepared for the registry of incidents, then a Microsoft Excel macro can read thousands of these spread sheets and build a trend line for risks in less than five minutes. Without this macro, (that is to say, an automated program), it would take the technology area hours or months to build programs which will very soon become obsolete.

In 2019, at the National Safety Council in San Diego, California I was surprised to see that no lecturer dealt with the subject of injury metrics, nobody talked about metrics combined with the use of temperature, humidity or weather sensors! At what temperature did accidents occur? Is there any behavioral pattern present there?. Let's think this: if we observe an Excel table with 5 columns, date, hour, type of injury and GPS location, environmental temperature at this location, and temperature or weather at this geographical area, are there any patterns showing the occurrence of events under certain circumstances?

It is estimated that the actual cost of injuries in the United States is equivalent to the 64% of each dollar derived from federal taxes and to a 56% of each dollar used to buy food.

Source: https://injuryfacts.nsc.org/

All preventable injuries, 2017

Class	Deaths	Change from 2014	Deaths per 100,000 people	Medically consulted injuries (a)
All classes (b)	169,936	5.3%	52.2	47,200,000
Motor vehicle	40,231	-0.2%	12.4	4,600,000
Public nonwork	38,210			4,400,000
Work	1,821			200,000
Home	200			(c)
Work	4,414	0.3%	1.4	4,500,000
Non-motor vehicle	2,593			4,300,000
Motor vehicle	1,821			200,000
Home	90,200	6.0%	27.7	25,300,000
Non-motor vehicle	90,000			25,300,000
Motor vehicle	200			(c)
Public	37,100	10.4%	11.4	13,000,000

Source: https://injuryfacts.nsc.org/

Technology and lone work

Lone work is one of the most hazardous tasks carried out in plants, for on many occasions there is no effective communication network enabling any kind of connection with this worker.

It is here where the need to have movable monitors such a drones, becomes evident. In presence of a risk pattern (for example, the appearance of a helmet in a risky area, an idle helmet when it should be moving, or a helmet that moves too quickly, to name a few) the drone can automatically monitor efficiently the worker´s situation.

Legal updating needs

As expected, due to the constant advance of technology, the corresponding legal frameworks are always behind action. Consequently, the need to update the legal framework quickly becomes evident. In Argentina, for example, the legal framework refers to the regulations of 1958 and decree 351 of the year 1979. No wonder how things have changed in the last 40 years....

Relying on permanent organizations, such as monitoring bodies for safety and health at the workplace, will become necessary due to the radical changes that will very soon start to take place as more and more technology is being incorporated to our activities.

Even if the greatest technological developments, which will later be beneficial for workers or society as a whole, start being top secret developments of the security forces for the defense of different countries, we must advocate for the immediate availability of these developments for the safety and health of workers. And not only this, we must also encourage the passing of new legislation.

It is also necessary to work hard to achieve the global standards of regulations and/or better industrial practices, for sometimes, it turns out to be very difficult to translate a regulation from one country to the other or from one region to another. This leads to impaired levels of compliance or to its poor implementation subject to each country's capability and not with the seriousness inherent to this subject.

We must work seriously to avoid any type of injury, mainly fatalities.

Human body analysis in depth

Understanding potential health risks at the workplace has always been my main concern. There are many really "invisible" symptoms which have direct impact on injuries and fatalities. If a person has a severe pain in the chest for many seconds, his attention on the task at hand will be impaired, giving place to a potential accident at that precise moment.

Every organization offers periodical medical check-ups to their employees, but lately DNA tests to evaluate ancestors and prevent diseases have acquired a growing importance.

In terms of health, I am worried about privacy when obtaining DNA information from saliva samples that can be sent by mail, but I also see that data privacy is a global challenge not confined to health but relative to all the aspects of life. Because of this, I would like to elaborate on the issue of privacy, as I think that governments and consumers have to work jointly to protect data.

I am really interested in the potential diagnosis resulting from this type of DNA test to prevent disease. Due to this, this year 2019 I have decided, together with my team, to analyze the services provided by the enterprise www.23andme.com

Even if results might not be accurate, they represent an important advance for the analysis of health risks. I will be surely interested, and that's why I refer in this book to the potential development of a genetic database in enterprises (without people's identification), related to certain characteristics of their workforce.

For this reason, I wanted to include this subject in this book published in the year 2019, so that I can compare in the years to come current reports with future developments.

Firstly, every service has a generic report of traits such as: bold (only for men), bunion, dandruff, early loss of hair (only for men), fear of heights, flat foot, mosquito bites frequency, kinetosis (an incongruity comes about between visually perceived movement and the vestibular system's sense of bodily movement), to name a few.

Health predisposition reports comprise the following:

- Diabetes type 2,(developed by 23andMeResearch, to analyze if the body produces or misuses insulin which helps glucose enter cells and provide energy.

- o Genetic probability of a disorder in the regulation of blood sugar levels.
- Macular degeneration associated with aging, which affects the macula, the part of the eye in charge of seeing small details.
  - o Genetic risk of any kind of vision impairment in adults.
  - o 2 variants in ARMS2 and CFH genes, used among other things, to analyze vision impairment with age.
- Alfa-1 antitrypsin, or ATT, protects lungs from inflammation due to infection or irritating substances inhaled.
  - o Genetic risk of lung and liver disease.
  - o 2 variants in the SERPINA1 gene, related with previously mentioned ATT.
- BRCA1 / BRCA2 (selected variants), genes that inhibit malignant tumors.
  - o Genetic risk based on a limited number of variants for breast, ovary and other types of cancer.
  - o 3 variants of BRCA1 and BRCA2 genes
- Celiac disease
  - o Genetic risk of autoimmune disorders associated to gluten.
  - o 2 variants of HLA-DQB1 and HLA-DQA1 genes, associated to celiac disease.
- Hypercholesterolemia in the family, to assess the risk of the presence of cholesterol in blood over normal parameters.
  - o Genetic risk of very high cholesterol, which might increase the risk of heart disease.

- o 24 variants in LDLR and APOB genes to analyze the risks of LDL cholesterol over normal parameters.
- G6PD deficiency, which mainly affect red blood cells, in charge of taking oxygen from the lungs to the body tissues.
    - o Genetic risk of a type of anemia.
    - o 1 variant in G6PD gene
    - o Hereditary Amyloidosis (associated to TTR), is a condition that generates abnormal deposits of protein in the body tissues, more frequently in the heart, kidneys and the nervous system.
    - o Genetic risk for a type of nervous and heart impairment.
    - o 3 variants in TTR gene.
- Hereditary Hemochromatosis (associated to HFE), to analyze high levels of iron in the body which hurt tissues and organs.
    - o Genetic risk of iron overload.
    - o 2 variants in HFE gene.
- Hereditary Thrombophilia, related to the possibility of forming abnormal blood clots.
    - o Genetic risk of harmful blood clots.
    - o 2 variants in F2 and F5 genes, related to blood coagulation disorders.
- Late Alzheimer´s.
    - o Genetic risk for a type of dementia.
    - o 1 variant of APOE gene.
- Polyposis associated to MUTYH
    - o Genetic risk of specific colorectal cancer.
    - o 2 variants of MUTYH gene.
- Parkinson´s disease.
    - o Genetic risk for a form of motor disability.

o 2 variants of LRRK2 and GBA genes.

They include health reports including alcohol discharge reaction, caffeine intake, deep sleep, genetic weight, lactose intolerance, muscle composition, saturated fat and weight and sleep movement.

There are many more reports which show deficiencies in D-functional protein related with the protection of enzymes in charge of energizing the body; others which show intolerance to fructose and various potential risks, which will also depend on people´s origins.

I want to state that this information can be incorrect and is taken from the internet only as illustrating material to show the potential of DNA analysis technology. It is my duty to work so that people enjoy good health, so I made reference to these analyses in this book of trends in the chapter dealing with measurements. If 80% of my employees have certain characteristics we have to assist them.

I did not want include further Information about the analyses, because some may be very important and others not that important, but I mention some of the analyses offered in October 2019 in 23andme website. I do not intend to offer a diagnosis of their use, but to share the curiosity I feel for the analyses that are coming once they become popular.

Future risks and strengths of genetic analyses

Future risks of genetic analyses include all the different types of discrimination that may be suffered according to the higher or lower predisposition to certain health disorders. But, on the other hand, they provide useful information for nutrition experts at enterprises.

I am convinced that, as food is the main source of energy of our body, in the future there will be a specific nutritional area reporting to operations, human resources and CSR divisions, in charge of corporate social responsibility. In my book on Corporate Social Responsibility, CSR I talked about its importance in detail.

Intellectual property, an invitation to add value to the future

When analyzing investment in safety, only a few production enterprises consider this analysis as a Source of income for the organization.

Production enterprises generally look for the easiest solution, the one at hand, they try to find a supplier who creates it and a service enterprise that sells it and provides training in it, but let's bear in mind that our personnel is an infinite source of real solutions.

It would be advisable, if we observe a methodology applied to our enterprises or the design of a useful object, to ask ourselves if there is any chance of registering the intellectual property of this methodology of use and/or design.

In practice, a patent has a cost of approximately 40,000 dollars, which covers its development, administrative, legal and professional paper work.

But, at an accounting level, most of these patents have a value in the enterprise assets and capital of more than a quarter million dollars per patent. A patent needs to have been registered for 20 years before it enters the public domain and it is then when we can license this technology to other enterprises generating additional income from intellectual property licenses.

In turn, if these patents generate maintenance tasks it is a cost, but generating related patents is useful to increase capital once more.

For this reason, generating patents brings about 3 sources of additional income when analyzing intellectual property:

a. Increase in capital, which in most cases increases the enterprise value.
b. Increase in income from additional profits from licensed intellectual property.
c. Increase in business opportunities.

We should add here, the motivation derived from being part of an organization where creativity and inventive are encouraged and appreciated. It is a common practice to mention the names of the employees who have created the patents, and this gives them prestige (patents belong to the enterprise, not to employees) and in general the prize for patents development is estimated in over 5,000 dollars each registration. These prizes are generally divided among the team participants who developed the patent.

Why is this subject important? Because an enterprise should also build its future, and to this end, innovation must be encouraged and supported. There are thousands of trainers who foster innovation and creativity, but only a few of them produced in their classroom, patents which had contributed significant improvements in Safety.

When we work on the future at my workshops and courses, I always invite participants to fill in creativity forms where ideas cannot be included, only methodologies and designs that have been put into practice. My style is to motivate concrete acts not just philosophical discussions about improvement.

Continuing with this analysis and also finishing this book, I want to share a 2-column exercise, similar to the ones done at my workshops: in the first column indicate a type of sensor you know, and in the second column indicate how you would incorporate it to personal protective elements and training.

Sensor, indicate a list of at least 20 sensors you know	Indicate one direct use of a specific personal protective element, one training use and one use combined with another sector.
Sensor:	PPE:
	Training:
	Combined use:
Sensor:	PPE:
	Training:
	Combined use:
Sensor:	PPE:
	Training:
	Combined use:
Sensor:	PPE:
	Training:

Combined use:

Sensor: PPE:

Training:

Combined use:

Sensor: PPE:

Training:

Combined use:

Sensor: PPE:

Training:

Combined use:

Sensor: PPE:

Training:

Combined use:

Sensor: PPE:

Training:

Combined use:

Sensor: PPE:

Training:

Combined use:

Sensor: PPE:

Training:

Combined use:

Sensor: PPE:

Training:

Combined use:

Sensor: PPE:

Training:

Combined use:

Sensor: PPE:

Training:

Combined use:

Sensor: PPE:

                                 Training:

                                 Combined use:

Sensor: PPE:

                                 Training:

                                 Combined use:

Sensor: PPE:

                                 Training:

                                 Combined use:

Sensor: PPE:

                                 Training:

                                 Combined use:

Sensor: PPE:

                                 Training:

                                 Combined use:

Sensor: PPE:

                                 Training:

                                 Combined use:

Sensor: PPE:

                                 Training:

                                 Combined use:

Sensor: PPE:

                                 Training:

                                 Combined use:

PART 4 AFTERTHOUGHTS & REFLEXIONS

A crisis occurs when the old does not finish dying and when the new is not yet born

Berlot Brecht

Why do crises happen and the end? April 2020 Reflections

All crises happen and then they go away because everything does, and all that remains is what we were able to build in both times of peace and in times **of turbulence..**

When we talk about issues of Safety it does not escape that law. Today more than ever, as leaders, we must be alert and vigilant about the health and safety of our people. And when I say our people, I mean our family, friends, work teams, neighbors, collaborators and ourselves.

Self-leadership in terms of safety has become, in this time of pandemic, an even more fundamental issue than it already was before. To not perceive the risk that surrounds us today without the seriousness and social consciousness necessary is a trap in which we can fall from considering the enemy an "invisible" one, as are many of the risks that surround us on our daily life. And that's why we let our guard down, because we don't see it or we get used to living with it, or we create to ourselves a false sense of safety where we make ourselves believe that things are ok, things are going well or things are getting better on their own.

And so, we allow ourselves to loosen up our defenses and common sense in the way of building the awareness of safety and health. That's a journey that does not have a happy ending.

To achieve some sort of happy ending in post of the caring of the most precious asset that we have, which is our life, we must work permanently in the search for continuous improvement.

Improving our organizational processes, improving our safety management processes, improving the safety culture and above all things improving our own skills as leaders and even more so as people, it is critical to be able to face the challenges of this new world that is brewing. It is true that every crisis brings new opportunities in return, but in order to take them you must be prepared.

We have in our hands the opportunity and responsibility to exercise our **visible leadership** in front of our people. We have the non-delegable responsibility for the caring of others that we implicitly accept when we claim to be their leader, their guide. The commitment then is to get into action. Let's do it!

Today more than ever our people need committed leaders, with courage and humanitarian skills and heart, ensuring the safety and health of their teams. Let's seize this moment. What we are living today is unique and historic. Let us work up to the circumstances and the needs of our people.

Many companies have the BCP -Business Continuity Plan- with crisis committees and emergency preparations. Such committees formulate simulations and tests of abnormal situations but under normal conditions. However, for the times that we live nowadays no one was prepared, and it is even more complex, since most people had not even thought about it.

Well, let me rephrase that last bit. The truth is that yes, many people in universities and government agencies thought about a scenario as the one we are living today. It was also thought by many creators of science fiction movies, but as something that can only happen in our imagination. Some lateral thinkers like Bill Gates talked about it in 2015, but he was taken as an exaggerated idea or very advanced in time.

And yet here we are, starting the year 2020 in which the worst pandemic in history has been declared. A microscopic entity, a virus, a Coronavirus, that scientists are still discussing whether a virus is a living being or not. And in the midst of all that discussion the virus is killing us and is killing the world, literally and not so literally speaking.

The worst deaths are the real ones, the deaths of thousands of real people, no doubt about it. However, before the situation normalizes, this global crisis will shake us with its aftershocks, as all great earthquakes do, that will be many and there will be plenty of other types of deaths.

Many things and dynamics will definitely change. Money and the relationship with money will change. Perhaps cryptocurrencies and virtual money will be kicked out of the investment portfolios of a few enlightened ones and get pushed into everyone's daily life in the rise of the world of the new order. That would prevent, for example, queues at banks, pharmacies and supermarkets.

Major and important changes in cleaning and hygiene rituals, both in businesses and homes, are changing and that change has come to stay.

And without a doubt what has changed forever is work. Everyone's work. Many of us resisted the virtual world, because the one-on-one contact was part of what we wanted to feel, we wanted to feel close to other people. Work will forever change as will many other experiences that we believed it could only be done by being physically present. Today´s reality confronts us with many of our limiting beliefs, many of which we live and experience in so many areas of our lives, and that are also to be found the area of safety.

The year 2020 came and from one day to the next, suddenly and in a blink of an eye, without asking permission or giving us time to organize anything, our home became our office. But not only our house was transformed into the office of all those who work in each home, but it was also transformed into a school, a kindergarten, a gym, a restaurant, a hair salon, everything!!! Our homes have been transformed into everything 7 days a week 24 hours a day. Many of us were brought a computer to our house the very next day and our children were no longer welcomed at their schools. At that very moment the real change began. Because in addition it was no longer allowed, nor was it safe, to leave our houses.

To work well we must have a space that accommodates all our needs and requirements of all kinds. That is why it is extremely important to have a safe, healthy and happy design and equipment for the home office workspace.

Let's look at several important points that we can contribute from the Safety area for this new stage of a home office:

Ergonomics

Ergonomics is the science that adapts the job to the activity and the person who develops it and not the other way around. Since the industrial revolution was always prioritized or played with the incredible adaptability that human beings have to everything..

Even viruses!! And then tasks arose at very high temperatures, with heavy materials, with forced positions based on that imposed carrot, sometimes wonderful, that drives us to believe that human beings can do everything.

However, revolutionary thinkers emerged and with them the concept of Corporate Social Responsibility (CSR), which made us see and understand that not everything should be done, even if possible.

Although the term was first coined in 1857, in Poland, it was in the 1970s, well into the 20th century, that ergonomics took its relevance as we know it today.

The objectives of ergonomics are:

- To reduce or eliminate occupational risks, labor accidents and diseases.
- To decrease physical, psychophysical and mental fatigue
- To increasing the efficiency of productive activities

The bases and laws of ergonomy are already established and tested, and by them it is understood that for the safe, healthy and happy design of the workplace, the following four principles must be taken into account:

1. **The locative risks**: i.e. the risks inherent in the workplace itself.
   - Detect loose objects
   - Don't stan on tables or chairs to reach objects
   - Close drawers to avoid bumps and stumbles, among others possible accidents.
2. **Ergonomic risks:** are those that arise when we neglect our bodies position during the execution of our work.

   - Take into consideration the importance of lighting, the more natural and direct, the better. Avoid irritating and uncomfortable reflections on work surfaces.

- o Arrange the more frequently used objects nearby and at your fingertips, and the least frequently used objects in a wider radius distance.
- o Keep your elbows and knees always at 90 degrees in relationship to the body axis.
- o Keep your feet firmly resting on the ground. To accomplish this, you can use shoe boxes, wooden drawers or cushions.
- o Keep the dorsal spine comfortably supported by the back of the chair (yes, you have to choose a chair with backrest), if you can't get your back to rest comfortably on the backrest you should try using some cushions.

3. **Electrical risks:** these are more common than we think and perhaps the least measured.
   - o To avoid them keep the cables neat and out of the way to avoid tripping and falling over
   - o Don't place glasses with water or infusions in places where you might inadvertently dump them on your keyboard or computer
   - o Don't overload plugs

- o Don´t use extenders that are not approved by a licensed electrician
- o Electrical installation, both at work, and at home must have differential protection and circuit breakers

4. **Psychosocial risks:** These have become more relevant today than ever before due to periods of obligatory social isolation, but it goes without saying that home office work has always been and always will be a challenge, especially regarding the maintenance of fluid and healthy interpersonal relationships, even more so during these special times.

Building happiness

In addition to everything mentioned above, it is important to have a work environment that makes us happy, that provides us with well-being, comfort and joy. And so, we must build that environment. Yes, build it. Because the environment that leads to happiness is built in all areas of life.

To build happiness we will use the science of positive psychology. This science ensures that 50% of the level of our happiness is due to our hereditary base, 10% is due to the circumstances and the remaining 40% is due to the intentional activities we do in our lives. That is why we can affirm that happiness is built, it is a choice that we can make. Science shows that we have a 40% of "space" to shape our lives with nice thoughts and feelings that come from doing things we like and makes us feel good.

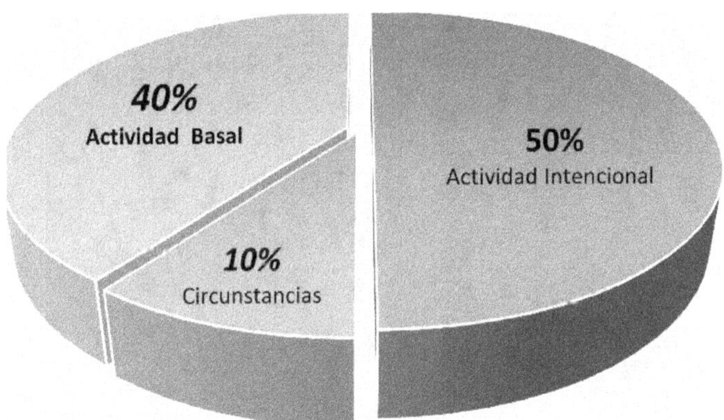

Another important part of our home office routine is being able to make **active micro breaks.**

Active micro active breaks or micro active pauses serve us to make some muscle stretching exercises. It is necessary to take them every certain interval of time to help prevent diseases typical of those who spend many hours in little or no movement and can expose us to two specific dangerous risks: sedentary lifestyle and non-ergonomic body posture.

Unlike an accident, which is a sudden and unexpected event, occupational diseases manifest over time, as they are the consequence of cumulative and gradual exposure to poor work habits.

Obviously, for an occupational disease to develop, an individual must also have a basal load of predisposition. There are people who, at the same stimulus, do not develop a disease that others do, or develop it later, or it manifests itself with less severity.

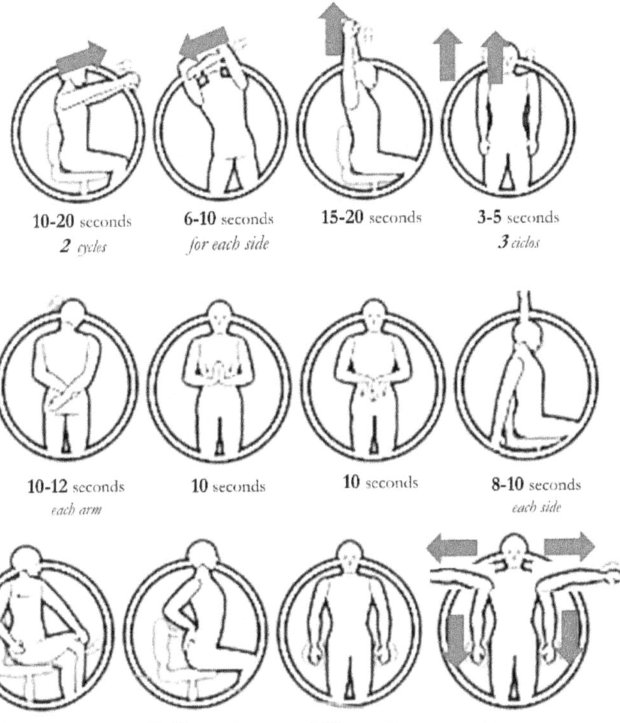

10-20 seconds
2 cycles

6-10 seconds
for each side

15-20 seconds

3-5 seconds
3 ciclos

10-12 seconds
each arm

10 seconds

10 seconds

8-10 seconds
each side

8-10 seconds
each side

10-15 seconds
2 cycles

6-20 seconds
shaking hands

10-20 seconds
strech the arms

Performing 3 to 5 minutes of micro-breaks every three to four hours of work will

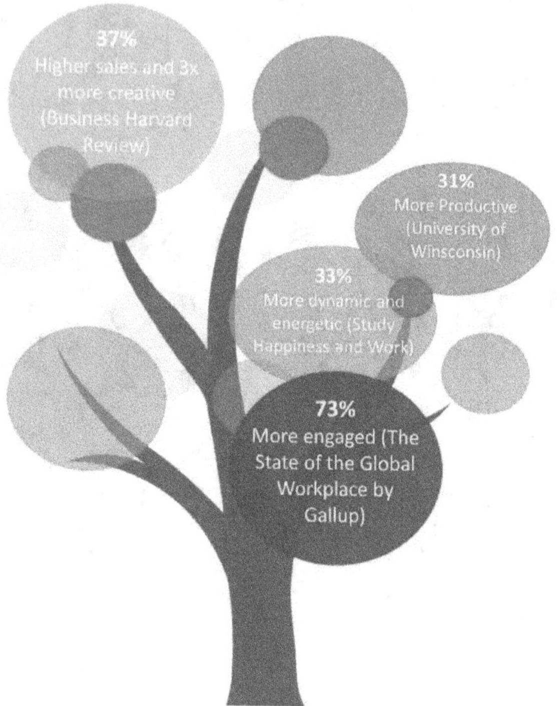

improve not only our body, but also our attention, our mood and our mood. Staying on the move is extremely important to our psychophysical balance.

Happy companies are those that make sure their employees are happy, because organizations are the sum of all their employees.

Human beings are a unique and indivisible entity, and from ontological coherence we are what we say, and that transforms us into what we do. To be happy we must think, feel, say and do in a coherent way, that is, harmoniously.

It's a good thing that many years ago we got rid of a very limiting belief that said that personal problems could be left at the entrance door of the office, or at the entrance gate of the factory, or in the entrance hall of the house next to the umbrella and the coat. Today we know that this is not the case anymore because it's neither possible nor healthy.

My reflection in this annex is purely to invite you to walk this path of coherence and allow emotions to emerge in the area that needs to emerge, thus avoiding much stress.

Stress

The workload that the employee believes they cannot handle is called job stress, and nowadays it is the second most important and frequent cause of work sick leave followed by musculoskeletal causes.

What is striking is that both causes, musculoskeletal and emotional, are affecting all industries and organizations without distinction of which category they belong to.

Today, in the midst of the Coronavirus pandemic spreading through our streets, the two most prevalent causes of sick leave are in full bloom.

We have the feeling that our bodies and minds have been imprisoned by an invisible enemy against which we cannot fight. But it's not like that. We can fight against it from what we know, which is to take care of our body with the tools that give us safety, hygiene, ergonomics and above all our minds, with the tools of positive psychology, creativity and mental flexibility.

.

Happy and healthy employees build happy and healthy organizations. Healthy organizations have been proven to be more efficient and profitable business. Therefore, it will be the organizations that understand this important concept and invest on it all their resources (human, capital, know-how, lateral thinking, etc.) the ones that will survive to these or any other time of crisis.

Epilogue

Writing about the future represents a real challenge, for we must generate useful conversation which leads to action and not philosophical non productive talking. I have been hearing about the importance of innovation and I have always intended, in case of writing about the future, to offer concrete actions as drivers for developing added value.

Only one patent is needed to demonstrate with facts, the importance of creative working. I plan to work with exercises that stimulate innovation without producing any concrete result.

And concrete results in innovation are achieved through stimulation and action oriented leadership. I am absolutely convinced that working on improved leadership brings about a virtuous chain of facts. Leadership, Social Responsibility, and future, a combination of three elements crucial to set the foundations of my fourth book, "Change Management".

I called this structure Lanfranchi´s quadrilateral, and it completes my Lanfranchi´s 2030 vision of zero Injuries.

It is necessary then to recommend the annual objectives performance assessment including all the subjects discussed in my books.

I thank you for joining me in this adventure into the future of safety and I invite you to engage in this mission with responsibility and with your coherent daily actions.

Please do not hesitate to contact me for further information or with your contribution, which will always be welcomed. To this end, you can write to me at debbie@resiliere.com or telephone my consulting office.

Deborah C. Lanfranchi

Experienced leader in HSE and Manufacturing with vast working background in multinational companies. Expert in Corporate Management Systems, Risk Management and ISO Standards. Certified Professional Coaching, Life Coaching. Chemical Engineer. UTN/UBA. Analyst of Safety Behavior Metrics. Associated to CPIQ.

Education

Chemical Engineering. Universidad Tecnológica Nacional – (Public University of Technology), Argentina.

Professional Ontolological Coaching.

Specialized in Industrial Safety and Hygiene – Universidad de Buenos Aires (University of Buenos Aires) – Argentina.

Former teacher at the Post-graduate course in Safety and Hygiene Specialization, School of Exact and Natural Sciences - Universidad de Buenos Aires (University of Buenos Aires) - Argentina.

NOTES

NOTES

NOTES

NOTES

NOTES

NOTES